The Wisdom and Wit
of
FRANKLIN D. ROOSEVELT

Edited By

PETER & HELEN BEILENSON

Illustrated By

JUNE MAGAZINER

PETER PAUPER PRESS, INC.

WHITE PLAINS • NEW YORK

"Let me assert my belief that the only thing we have to fear is fear itself."

Franklin Delano Roosevelt (1882-1945) led our nation for 13 years through one of the most difficult periods in its history. His wisdom and wit gave Americans the strength and encouragement to persevere throughout the Great Depression. Similarly, his Fireside Chats and other speeches instilled pride and confidence in the American people as, at home and abroad, the Nation waged World War II.

FDR's words — still extremely relevant today — evoke the same emotional response in the face of our current economic, international, and spiritual problems. It is, in part, because his remarks have such lasting importance that Franklin Delano Roosevelt is viewed as one of our Nation's great Presidents.

We hope you enjoy this representative collection of "quotes" from FDR!

The Editors

On America

The overwhelming majority of Americans are possessed of two great qualities — a sense of humor and a sense of proportion.

This Nation is not merely a Nation of independence but it is, if we are to survive, bound to be a Nation of interdependence — town and city, and North and South, East and West.

.   .   .

No man of my generation has any business to address youth unless he comes to the task not in the spirit of exultation, but in a spirit of humility.

5

It is not unkind to say, from the standpoint of scenery alone, that if many, and indeed most, of our American national parks were to be set down on the continent of Europe thousands of Americans would journey all the way across the ocean in order to see their beauties.

.   .   .

I do not look upon these United States as a finished product. We are still in the making.

.   .   .

The history of every nation is eventually written in the way it cares for its soil.   *Statement on signing Soil Conservation Act,   1936*

.   .   .

Many older people seem to take unmerited pride in the mere fact that they are adults.   *Address to Young Democratic Club 1936*

6

This generation of Americans has a rendezvous with destiny.

*   *   *

The school is the last expenditure upon which America should be willing to economize.

*   *   *

I believe, I have always believed, and I will always believe in private enterprise as the backbone of economic well-being in the United States.

*   *   *

The struggle against private monopoly is a struggle for, and not against American business. It is a struggle to preserve individual enterprise and economic freedom.

*   *   *

No man can sever the bonds that unite him to his society simply by averting his eyes.

7

We are all bound together by hope of a common future rather than by reverence for a common past . . . For all our millions of square miles, for all our millions of people, there is a unity in language and speech, in law and in economics, in education and in general purpose which nowhere finds its match.

.   .   .

For over three centuries a steady stream of men, women, and children followed the beacon of liberty which this light symbolizes. They brought to us strength and moral fibre developed in a civilization centuries old, but fired anew by the dream of a better life in America. They brought to one new country the cultures of a hundred old ones. *Address on the Fiftieth Anniversary of the Statue of Liberty 1936*

.   .   .

The people of America are in agreement in defending their liberties at any cost, and the first line of that defense lies in the protection of economic security.

Once I prophesied that this generation of Americans had a rendezvous with destiny. That prophecy now comes true. To us much is given; more is expected. *Annual Message to Congress, 1939*

.   .   .

We have our difficulties, true—but we are a wiser and a tougher nation than we were in 1929, or in 1932. *Annual Message to Congress, 1939*

.   .   .

It has been aptly suggested that its [the government of the United States] successful organizing should rank as the eighth wonder of the world—for surely the evolution of permanent substance out of nebulous chaos justifies us in the use of superlatives. *Address on the One Hundred and Fiftieth Anniversary of Congress, 1939*

.   .   .

Whoever seeks to set one religion against another seeks to destroy all religion.

9

For more than three centuries we Americans have been building on this continent a free society . . . we have built well. We are continuing our efforts to bring the blessings of a free society, of a free and productive economic system, to every family in the land. This is the promise of America.

.   .   .

We have always held to the hope, the belief, the conviction, that there is a better life, a better world, beyond the horizon.

.   .   .

The Americas have excelled in the adventure of many races living together in harmony.

.   .   .

It seems to me that we are most completely, most loudly, most proudly American around an election day.

Always the heart and the soul of our country will be the heart and the soul of the common man—the men and the women who never have ceased to believe in democracy, who never have ceased to love their families, their homes, and their country.

·   ·   ·

We have more faith in the collective opinion of all Americans than in the individual opinion of any one American.

·   ·   ·

Freedom means the supremacy of human rights everywhere. Our support goes to those who struggle to gain those rights and keep them. Our strength is our unity of purpose.

·   ·   ·

This land is great because it is a land of endless challenge.

As a nation we may take pride in the fact that we are soft-hearted; but we can not afford to be soft-headed. We must always be wary of those who with sounding brass and a tinkling cymbal preach the ism of appeasement. We must especially beware of that small group of selfish men who would clip the wings of the American eaglet to feather their own nests. *1941*

. . .

On each national day of inauguration since 1789, the people have renewed their sense of dedication to the United States.

In Washington's day the task of the people was to create and weld together a nation.

In Lincoln's day the task of the people was to preserve that nation from disruption from within.

In this day the task of the people is to save the nation and its institutions from disruptions from without. *Third Inaugural Address, 1941*

Lives of nations are determined not by the count of years, but by the lifetime of the human spirit. The life of a man is threescore years and ten; a little more, a little less. The life of a nation is the fullness of the measure of its will to live.

.　　.　　.

A nation, like a person, has a body— a body that must be fed and clothed and housed, invigorated and rested, in a manner that measures up to the standards of our time.

A nation like a person, has a mind—a mind that must be kept informed and alert, that must know itself, that understands the hopes and needs of its neighbors—all the other nations that live within the narrowing circle of the world.

A nation, like a person, has something deeper, something more permanent, something larger than the sum of its parts. It is that something which matters most to its future, which calls forth the most sacred guarding of its present.

Art is not a treasure in the past or an importation from another land, but part of the present life of all the living and creating peoples.   *Dedication Address, National Gallery of Art, 1941*

.   .   .

It is our duty to make sure that, big as this country is, there is no room for racial or religious intolerance—and that there is no room for snobbery.

.   .   .

America must remain the land of high wages and efficient production. Every full-time job in America must provide enough for a decent living.

.   .   .

America has always been a land of action—a land of adventurous pioneering—a land of growing and building: America must always be such a land.   *1944*

15

The Depression
And
The New Deal

I pledge you—I pledge myself to a new deal for the American people.   *Acceptance Speech, Democratic National Convention, 1932*

No political party has exclusive patent rights on prosperity.

.   .   .

A real economic cure must go to the killing of bacteria in the system rather than the treatment of external symptoms.   *1932*

Let us all here assembled constitute ourselves prophets of a new order of competence and of courage. This is more than a political campaign; it is a call to arms. Give me your help, not to win votes alone, but to win in this crusade to restore America to its own people. *Acceptance Speech, Democratic National Convention, 1932*

.   .   .

Out of every crisis, every tribulation, every disaster, mankind rises with some share of greater knowledge, of higher decency, of purer purpose.

.   .   .

Save homes; save homes for thousands of self-respecting families, and drive out that spectre of insecurity from our midst. *1932*

.   .   .

Idle factories and idle workers profit no man.

18

What do the people of America want more than anything else? In my mind, two things: Work; work, with all the moral and spiritual values that go with work. And with work, a reasonable measure of security—security for themselves and for their wives and children. Work and security—these are more than words. They are more than facts. They are the spiritual values, the true goal toward which our efforts of reconstruction should lead. *1932*

. . .

Statesmanship and vision, my friends, require relief to all at the same time.

. . .

Wild radicalism has made few converts, and the greatest tribute that I can pay to my countrymen is that in these days of crushing want there persists an orderly and hopeful spirit on the part of the millions of our people who have suffered so much. To fail to offer them a new chance is not only to betray their hopes but to misunderstand their patience. *1932*

19

Every man has a right to life; and this means that he has also a right to make a comfortable living. He may by sloth or crime decline to exercise that right; but it may not be denied him.

. . .

This is preeminently the time to speak the truth, the whole truth, frankly and boldly. Nor need we shrink from honestly facing conditions in our country today. This great Nation will endure as it has endured, will revive and will prosper. So, first of all, let me assert my firm belief that the only thing we have to fear is fear itself—nameless, unreasoning, unjustified terror which paralyzes needed efforts to convert retreat into advance. In every dark hour of our national life a leadership of frankness and vigor has met with that understanding and support of the people themselves which is essential to victory. I am convinced that you will again give that support to leadership in these critical days.   *First Inaugural Address, 1933*

This Nation asks for action, and action now. *First Inaugural Address, 1933*

.   .   .

The money changers have fled from their high seats in the temple of our civilization. We may now restore that temple to the ancient truths. The measure of the restoration lies in the extent to which we apply social values more noble than mere monetary profit.

.   .   .

When Andrew Jackson, "Old Hickory," died, someone asked, "Will he go to Heaven," and the answer was, "He will if he wants to." If I am asked whether the American people will pull themselves out of this depression, I answer, "They will if they want to."

.   .   .

We have all suffered in the past from individualism run wild.

21

A thinking America . . . seeks a Government of its own that will be sufficiently strong to protect the prisoner and at the same time to crystallize a public opinion so clear that Government of all kinds will be compelled to practice a more certain justice. The judicial function of government is the protection of the individual and of the community through quick and certain justice. That function in many places has fallen into a sad state of disrepair. It must be a part of our program to reestablish it.   *1933*

.   .   .

The Administration needs and will tirelessly seek the best ability that the country affords. Public service offers better rewards in the opportunity for service than ever before in our history—not great salaries, but enough to live on. In the building of this service there are coming to us men and women with ability and courage from every part of the Union.

The primary concern of any Government dominated by the humane ideals of democracy is the simple principle that in a land of vast resources no one should be permitted to starve.

．　　　．　　　．

Our new structure is part of and a fulfillment of the old.

．　　　．　　　．

We find our population suffering from old inequalities, little changed by sporadic remedies. In spite of our efforts and in spite of our talk, we have not weeded out the over-privileged and we have not effectively lifted up the under-privileged. Both of these manifestations of injustice have retarded happiness. No wise man has any intention of destroying what is known as the profit motive: because by the profit motive we mean the right to work to earn a decent livelihood for ourselves and our families.

23

The simplest way for each of you to judge recovery lies in the plain facts of your own individual situation. Are you better off than you were last year? Are your debts less burdensome? Is your bank account more secure? Are your working conditions better? Is your faith in your own individual future more firmly grounded?   *1934*

.   .   .

Your Government has had but one sign on its desk—"Seek only the greater good of the greater number of Americans."

.   .   .

Overproduction, underproduction, and speculation are three evil sisters who distill the troubles of unsound inflation and disastrous deflation.

.   .   .

The statute of NRA has been outlawed. The problems have not. They are still with us.   *Annual Message to Congress, 1937*

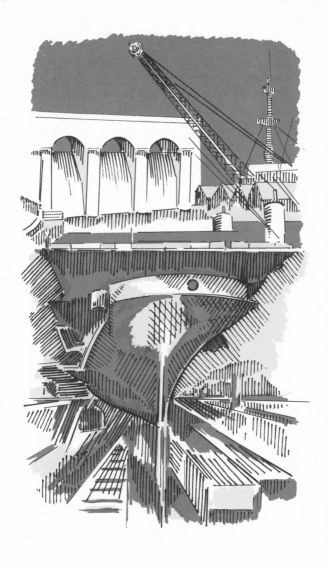

Americans must foreswear that conception of the acquisition of wealth which, through excessive profits, creates undue private power over private affairs, and to our misfortune, over public affairs as well. In building toward this end we do not destroy ambition nor do we seek to divide our wealth into equal shares on stated occasions. We continue to recognize the greater ability of some to earn more than others. But we do assert that the ambition of the individual to obtain for him and his a proper security, a reasonable leisure, and a decent living throughout life, is an ambition to be preferred to the appetite for great wealth and great power.

.   .   .

Our nation so richly endowed with natural resources and with a capable and industrious population should be able to devise ways and means of insuring to all our able-bodied working men and women a fair day's pay for a fair day's work.

Some economists are still trying to find out what it was that hit us back in 1929. I am not a professional economist but I think I know. What hit us was a decade of debauch, of group selfishness—the sole objective expressed in the thought—''every man for himself and the devil take the hindmost.'' And the result was that about 98 percent of the American population turned out to be ''the hindmost.'' *1936*

.   .   .

Today we reconsecrate our country to long cherished ideals in a suddenly-changed civilization. In every land there are always at work forces that drive men apart and forces that draw men together. In our personal ambitions we are individualists. But in our seeking for economic and political progress as a nation, we all go up—or else all go down—as one people. *Second Inaugural Address, 1937*

Government
And Democracy

Democracy cannot succeed unless those who express their choice are prepared to choose wisely. The real safeguard of democracy, therefore, is education.

What is the State? It is the duly constituted representative of an organized society of human beings, created by them for their mutual protection and well-being.

·   ·   ·

Our Government is not the master, but the creature of the people. The duty of the State toward the citizens is the duty of the servant to its master. The people have created it; the people, by common consent, permit its continual existence.

When people carelessly or snobbishly deride political parties, they overlook the fact that the party system of government is one of the greatest methods of unification and of teaching people to think in common terms of our civilization.

．　　　．　　　．

I say that while primary responsibility for relief rests with localities now, as ever, yet the Federal Government has always had and still has a continuing responsibility for the broader public welfare. *Acceptance Speech, Democratic National Convention, 1932*

．　　　．　　　．

Our Constitution is so simple and practical that it is possible always to meet extraordinary needs by changes in emphasis and arrangement without loss of essential form. That is why our constitutional system has proved itself the most superbly enduring political mechanism the modern world has produced.

Public office means serving the public and nobody else.

. . .

No group and no government can properly prescribe precisely what should constitute the body of knowledge with which true education is concerned.

. . .

Having tasted the benefits of liberation, men and women do not long forego those benefits.

. . .

Liberty requires opportunity to make a living—a living decent according to the standard of the time, a living which gives a man not only enough to live by, but something to live for.

. . .

There is no indispensable man.

31

We still find inspiration for the work before us, in the old frontier spirit which meant achievement through self-reliance; a willingness to lend a hand to the fellow down in his luck through no fault of his own. Upon those principles our democracy was reborn a century ago; upon those principles alone will it endure.

.   .   .

The basic things expected by our people of their political and economic system are simple. They are:

Equality of opportunity for youth and for others.

Jobs for those who can work.

Security for those who need it.

The ending of special privilege for the few.

The preservation of civil liberties for all.

The employment of the fruits of scientific progress in a wider and constantly rising standard of living.

Federal laws supplementing State laws are needed to help solve the problems which result from modern invention applied in an industrialized Nation which conducts its business with scant regard to State lines.

.　　.　　.

We are determined to make every American citizen the subject of his country's interest and concern; and we will never regard any faithful, law-abiding group within our borders as superfluous.

.　　.　　.

No government can help the destinies of people who insist in putting sectional and class consciousness ahead of general weal.

.　　.　　.

Not only our future economic soundness but the very soundness of our democratic institutions depends on the determination of our Government to give employment to idle men.

We want a Supreme Court which will do justice under the Constitution—not over it. In our Courts we want a government of laws and not of men. *Fireside Chat on the Plan to Reorganize the Judiciary, 1937*

.   .   .

This plan will save our National Constitution from hardening of the Judicial arteries. *Fireside Chat on the Plan to Reorganize the Judiciary, 1937*

.   .   .

I hope you have re-read the Constitution of the United States in these past few weeks. Like the Bible, it ought to be read again and again.

.   .   .

Those who do not like democracy want to keep legislators at home.

34

For a President especially it is a duty to think in national terms.

.   .   .

I am constantly thinking of all our people—unemployed and employed alike—of their human problems of food and clothing and homes and education and health and old age. *Fireside Chat, 1938*

.   .   .

I never forget that I live in a house owned by all the American people and that I have been given their trust . . . I want to be sure that neither battles nor burdens of office shall ever blind me to an intimate knowledge of the way the American people want to live and the simple purposes they put me here for.

.   .   .

People who are hungry and out of a job are the stuff of which dictatorships are made.

Sometimes I get bored sitting in Washington hearing certain people talk and talk about all that government ought not do, people who got all they wanted from government back in the days when the financial institutions and the railroads were being bailed out by the government in 1933. It is refreshing to go out through the country and feel the common wisdom that the time to repair the roof is when the sun is shining.   *Fireside Chat, 1937*

.   .   .

I am still convinced that the American people, since 1932, continue to insist on two requisites of private enterprise. The first is complete honesty at the top in looking after other people's money, and in apportioning and paying individual and corporate taxes according to ability to pay. The second is sincere respect for the need of all at the bottom to get work—and through work to get a really fair share of the good things of life, and a chance to save and rise.   *1938*

The millions of today want, and have a right to, the same security their forefathers sought—the assurance that with health and the willingness to work they will find a place for themselves in the social and economic system of the time.   *Radio Address on Social Security, 1938*

.   .   .

Books may be burned and cities sacked, but truth, like the yearning for freedom, lives in the hearts of humble men and women. The ultimate victory of tomorrow is with democracy, and through democracy with education, for no people in all the world can be kept eternally ignorant or eternally enslaved.

.   .   .

Nobody will ever deprive the American people of the right to vote except the American people themselves—and the only way they could do that is by not voting.

Religion, by teaching man his relationship to God, gives the individual a sense of his own dignity and teaches him to respect himself by respecting his neighbors.

Democracy, the practice of self-government, is a covenant among free men to respect the rights and liberties of their fellows.

International good faith, a sister of democracy, springs from the will of civilized nations of men to respect the rights and liberties of other nations of men.

In a modern civilization, all three—religion, democracy, and international good faith—complement and support each other.

.   .   .

Representative democracy will never tolerate suppression of true news at the behest of government.

.   .   .

Investment for prosperity can be made in a democracy.

The more I have studied American history and the more clearly I have seen what the problems are, I do believe that the common denominator of our great men in public life has not been mere allegiance to one political party, but the disinterested devotion with which they have tried to serve the whole country, and the relative unimportance that they ascribe to politics, compared with the paramount importance of Government.

.   .   .

Dictatorship involves costs which the American people will never pay: The cost of our spiritual values. The cost of the blessed right of being able to say what we please. The cost of freedom of religion. The cost of being cast into a concentration camp. The cost of being afraid to walk down the street with the wrong neighbor. The cost of having our children brought up, not as free and dignified human beings, but as pawns molded and enslaved by a machine.

In the period of thirty years, during which I have been more or less in public life . . . I have come to the conclusion that the closer people are to what may be called the front lines of Government, of all kinds—Local and State and Federal—the easier it is to see the immediate underbrush, the individual tree trunks of the moment, and to forget the nobility, the usefulness, and the wide extent of the forest itself.

.　　.　　.

Investing soundly must preclude spending wastefully.

.　　.　　.

Democracy can thrive only when it enlists the devotion of those whom Lincoln called the common people. Democracy can hold that devotion only when it adequately respects their dignity by so ordering society as to assure to the masses of men and women reasonable security and hope for themselves and for their children.

Freedom of speech is of no use to the man who has nothing to say . . . Freedom of worship is of no use to the man who has lost his God . . . A free election is of no use to the man who is too indifferent to vote.

.   .   .

We have come through a hard struggle to preserve democracy in America. Where other Nations in other parts of the world have lost that fight, we have won.

.   .   .

The deeper purpose of democratic government is to assist as many of its citizens as possible, especially those who need it most, to improve their conditions of life, to retain all personal liberty which does not adversely affect their neighbors, and to pursue the happiness which comes with security and an opportunity for recreation and culture.

A radical is a man with both feet firmly planted—in the air. A conservative is a man with two perfectly good legs who, however, has never learned to walk forward. A reactionary is a somnambulist walking backwards. A liberal is a man who uses his legs and his hands at the behest . . . of his head.

.　　　.　　　.

Eternal truths will be neither true nor eternal unless they have fresh meaning for every new social situation.

.　　　.　　　.

Democracy is the one form of society which guarantees to every new generation of men the right to imagine and to attempt to bring to pass a better world.

.　　　.　　　.

The only limit to our realization of tomorrow will be our doubts of today. *Undelivered Address, to have been given April 13, 1945*

War and Peace

Truly, if the genius of mankind that has invented the weapons of death cannot discover the means of preserving peace, civilization as we know it lives in an evil day.

In the field of world policy, I would dedicate this Nation to the policy of the good neighbor—the neighbor who resolutely respects himself and, because he does so, respects the rights of others—the neighbor who respects his obligations and respects the sanctity of his agreements in and with a world of neighbors.   *First Inaugural Address, 1933*

A selfish victory is always destined to be an ultimate defeat.   *1933*

.   .   .

The primary purpose of the United States of America is to avoid being drawn into war. We seek also in every practicable way to promote peace and to discourage war.

.   .   .

Let no man or woman forget that there is no profit in war. Sacrifices in the cause of peace are infinitesimal compared with the holocaust of war.

.   .   .

There is a solidarity and interdependence about the modern world, both technically and morally, which makes it impossible for any nation completely to isolate itself from economic and political upheavals in the rest of the world, especially when such upheavals appear to be spreading and not declining.

America hates war. America hopes for peace. Therefore, America actively engages in the search for peace.

. . .

The peace-loving nations must make a concerted effort in opposition to those violations of treaties and those ignorings of humane instincts which today are creating a state of international anarchy and instability from which there is no escape through mere isolation or neutrality.

. . .

We cannot and must not build walls around ourselves and hide our heads in the sand, we must go forward with all our strength to stress and strive for international peace.   *1935*

. . .

It seems to be unfortunately true that the epidemic of world lawlessness is spreading.

47

No nation which refuses to exercise forbearance and to respect the freedom and rights of others can long remain strong and retain the confidence and respect of other nations. No nation ever loses its dignity or its good standing by conciliating its differences, and by exercising great patience with, and consideration for, the rights of other nations.

. . .

Those who cherish their freedom and recognize and respect the equal right of their neighbors to be free and live in peace, must work together for the triumph of law and moral principles in order that peace, justice, and confidence may prevail in the world.

. . .

Of all the devastations of war none is more tragic than the destruction which it brings to the processes of men's minds. Truth is denied because emotion pushes it aside. Forbearance is succeeded by bitterness.

I want our great democracy to be wise enough to realize that aloofness from war is not promoted by unawareness of war. In a world of mutual suspicions, peace must be affirmatively reached for. It cannot just be wished for. It cannot just be waited for.

．　　　．　　　．

I have said not once, but many times, that I have seen war and that I hate war. I say that again and again.

．　　　．　　　．　　　．

The united strength of a democratic nation can be mustered only when its people, educated by modern standards to know what is going on and where they are going, have conviction that they are receiving as large a share of opportunity for development, as large a share of material success and of human dignity, as they have a right to receive.

Events abroad have made it increasingly clear to the American people that dangers within are less to be feared than dangers from without. *1939*

. . .

We must be the great arsenal of democracy.

. . .

The most dangerous enemies of American peace are those who, without well-rounded information on the whole broad subject of the past, the present, and the future, undertake to speak with assumed authority, to talk in terms of glittering generalities, to give the nation assurances or prophecies which are of little present or future value.

. . .

This Nation will remain a neutral Nation, but I cannot ask that every American remain neutral in thought as well. *1939*

50

One peaceful nation after another has met disaster because each refused to look the Nazi danger squarely in the eye, until it actually had them by the throat.

The United States will not make that fatal mistake.   *1941*

.   .   .

We know enough by now to realize that it would be suicide to wait until they are in our front yard.

When your enemy comes at you in a tank or a bombing plane, if you hold your fire until you see the whites of his eyes, you will never know what hit you. Our Bunker Hill of tomorrow may be several thousand miles from Boston.   *1941*

.   .   .

When you see a rattlesnake poised to strike, you do not wait until he has struck to crush him.

.   .   .

War is a contagion.

51

It would be unworthy of a great nation to exaggerate an isolated incident, or to become inflamed by some one act of violence.

．　　　．　　　．

In the future days, which we seek to make secure, we look forward to a world founded upon four essential human freedoms.

The first is freedom of speech and expression—everywhere in the world.

The second is freedom of every person to worship God in his own way—everywhere in the world.

The third is freedom from want—which, translated into world terms, means economic understandings which will secure to every nation a healthy, peacetime life for its inhabitants—everywhere in the world.

The fourth is freedom from fear—which, translated into world terms, means a world-wide reduction of armaments to such a point and in such a thorough fashion that no nation will be in a position to commit an act of physical aggression against any neighbor—anywhere in the world.
Four Freedoms Speech, January 6, 1941

History cannot be rewritten by wishful thinking.

.   .   .

Your Government has the right to expect of all citizens that they take loyal part in the common work of our common defense.

.   .   .

Yesterday, December 7, 1941—a date which will live in infamy—the United States of America was suddenly and deliberately attacked by naval and air forces of the Empire of Japan.   *War Message to Congress, 1941*

.   .   .

We are now in the midst of a war, not for conquest, not for vengeance, but for a world in which this Nation, and all that this Nation represents, will be safe for our children.   *Fireside Chat on Entrance to War, 1941*

It is not a sacrifice for any man, old or young, to be in the Army or the Navy of the United States. Rather, it is a privilege. *Pearl Harbor Speech to Congress, 1941*

. . .

No honest person, today or a thousand years hence, will be able to suppress a sense of indignation and horror at the treachery committed by the military dictators of Japan, under the very shadow of the flag of peace borne by their special envoys in our midst.

. . .

We are fighting today for security, for progress, and for peace, not only for ourselves but for all men, not only for one generation, but for all generations. We are fighting to cleanse the world of ancient evils, ancient ills.

There never has been—there never can be—successful compromise between good and evil. Only total victory can reward the champions of tolerance and decency and freedom and faith.

.   .   .

Here are three high purposes for every American:

1. We shall not stop work for a single day. If any dispute arises we shall keep on working while the dispute is solved by mediation, conciliation, or arbitration— until the war is won.

2. We shall not demand special gains or special privileges or advantages for any one group or occupation.

3. We shall give up conveniences and modify the routine of our lives if our country asks us to do so. We will do it cheerfully, remembering that the common enemy seeks to destroy every home and every freedom in every part of our land.

Battles are not won by soldiers or sailors who think first of their own personal safety. And wars are not won by people who are concerned primarily with their own comfort, their own convenience, their own pocket-books.

.　　.　　.

This whole nation of 130 million free men and women and children is becoming one great fighting force. Some of us are soldiers or sailors, some of us are civilians. Some of us are fighting the war in airplanes five miles above the continent of Europe or the Islands of the Pacific—and some of us are fighting in mines deep down in the earth of Pennsylvania or Montana. A few of us are decorated with medals for heroic achievement, but all of us can have that deep and permanent inner satisfaction that comes from doing the best we know how—each of us playing an honorable part in the great struggle to save our democratic civilization.

Today the whole world is one neighborhood . . . And unless the peace . . . recognizes that the whole world is one neighborhood and does justice to the whole human race, the germs of another World War will remain a constant threat to mankind.

.   .   .

The Axis Powers know that they must win the war in 1942—or eventually lose everything. I do not need to tell you that our enemies did not win this war in 1942. *State of the Union 1943*

.   .   .

We all know that books burn—yet we have the greater knowledge that books cannot be killed by fire. People die, but books never die. No man and no force can abolish memory. No man and no force can put thought in a concentration camp forever. No man and no force can take from the world the books that embody man's eternal fight against tyranny of every kind. In this war, we know, books are weapons . . . weapons for man's freedom.

It is one of our war aims, as expressed in the Atlantic Charter, that the conquered populations of today be again the masters of their destiny. There must be no doubt anywhere that it is the unalterable purpose of the United Nations to restore to conquered peoples their sacred rights.

.   .   .

We shall not settle for less than total victory. That is the determination of every American on the fighting fronts. That must be, and will be, the determination of every American here at home.

.   .   .

The tragedy of the war has sharpened the vision of the leadership and peoples of all the United Nations, and I can say to you from my own full knowledge that they see the utter necessity of our standing together after the war to secure a peace based on principles of permanence.

It has been our steady policy—and it is certainly a common sense policy—that the right of each nation to freedom must be measured by the willingness of that nation to fight for freedom.

.   .   .

It is our duty now to begin to lay plans and determine the strategy for the winning of a lasting peace and the establishment of an American standard of living higher than ever before known.   *1944*

.   .   .

Nations, like individuals, do not always see alike or think alike, and international cooperation and progress are not helped by any nation assuming that it has a monopoly of wisdom or of virtue.

.   .   .

The one supreme objective for the future . . . can be summed up in one word: Security.   *1944*

The structure of world peace cannot be the work of one man, or one party, or one nation. It cannot be an American peace, or a British peace, or a Russian peace, or a French or a Chinese peace. It cannot be a peace of large nations—or of small nations. It must be a peace which rests on the cooperative effort of the whole world.

.　　.　　.

Peace can endure only so long as humanity really insists upon it, and is willing to work for it—and sacrifice for it.

.　　.　　.

We seek peace—enduring peace. More than an end to war, we want an end to the beginnings of all wars—yes, an end to this brutal, inhuman, and thoroughly impractical method of settling the differences between governments. . . .   *Undelivered Address to have been given April 13, 1945*